HOW TO WRITE
STORIES

CELIA WARREN

QEB Publishing, Inc.

QEB

Copyright © QEB Publishing, Inc. 2007

First published in the United States by
QEB Publishing, Inc.
23062 La Cadena Drive
Laguna Hills, CA 92653

www.qeb-publishing.com

Library of Congress Control Number: 2007000924

ISBN 978-1-59566-343-6

Written by Celia Warren
Designed by Jackie Palmer
Editor Louisa Somerville
Illustrations by Tim Loughead
Consultant Anne Faundez

Publisher Steve Evans
Creative Director Zeta Davies
Senior Editior Hannah Ray

Printed and bound in the United States of America

Web site information is correct at time of going to press.
However, the publishers cannot accept liability for any
information or links found on third-party Web sites.

Words in **bold** are explained
in the glossary on page 30.

CONTENTS

STORY GENRES

Anyone who makes up stories and writes them down is an **author**. You can be an author, too! The wonderful thing about being an author is that you can be anyone, go anywhere, and do anything you like. If you want to sprout wings and fly or be a deep-sea diver, you can! You can do anything in your imagination. If you write a made-up story, it's called **fiction**. Take a look at some of the other **genres** of writing—but don't forget, some books can fit into more than one genre.

- **Fairy tales, legends, and folktales**
  Well-known traditional tales—including *Goldilocks and the Three Bears* and *The Frog Prince*—and **legends** such as those featuring Robin Hood and Odysseus.

- **Fables and parables**
  Stories with a moral or a message, including such Bible stories as *The Prodigal Son* and *The Good Shepherd*, and Aesop's **fables**, such as *The Tortoise and the Hare*.

- **Historical**
  Stories set in the past, such as *Out of the Dust* by Karen Hesse. They can be about real or fictional events.

Some authors' fictional **characters** are so convincing that they become as much a part of life as if they were real people. You'd know Winnie the Pooh, Alice in Wonderland, or Harry Potter if you met them in the street, wouldn't you?

- **Sci-fi (short for science fiction)**
  Stories inspired by scientific developments. They are usually set in the future and often involve aliens. The *Artemis Fowl* books by Eoin Colfer are sci-fi stories.

- **Fantasy**
  Stories whose characters or events are not based on reality. The reader must accept the writer's **fantasy** world. *The Lion, the Witch and the Wardrobe*, written by C.S. Lewis, is a fantasy story.

- **Adventure and mystery**
  Stories about exciting or mysterious events, in which readers try to follow the action along with the characters. *From the Mixed-Up Files of Mrs. Basil E. Frankweiler* by E. L. Konigsburg is a mystery story.

Tips
- It's often best to write the sort of story that you would enjoy reading yourself.
- Read as many books in different genres as you can. The more you read, the more your own writing will improve.

- **Graphic stories**
  Stories told in pictures, such as those about the adventures of Tintin or Asterix, in which the words are in speech bubbles and captions.

GATHERING IDEAS

Ideas for stories are everywhere. Something you see, hear, or dream may spark inspiration for a story or, at least, an event or a character. It's not always convenient to sit down and write a whole story immediately, so make notes when ideas occur to you.

Writer's notebook

Keep a notebook handy—with a pen, of course. Use it to jot down anything that pops into your head, even if it's just a word. It could come in handy when creating a character or situation for a new story. You could write down:

- an overheard snippet of conversation (but don't eavesdrop!)
- parts of dreams—as soon as you wake up.
- something funny, unusual, or interesting you see while walking in the park, such as a parent training a dog to find her children, a kite getting stuck in a tree, or a child's ice cream falling on a toddler's head.
- a series of words that pop into your head from nowhere, for example:

"Floppy poppy!
Well, blow me down!"

Tip

The next time you're in the mood to write, open your writer's notebook and see what you scribbled down—you'll probably find seeds of story ideas. Now you can "water" the seeds and watch them grow!

In the news

Newspapers are a great source for story ideas. Most news stories involve people (who can become your characters). For example, a new planet is discovered. Who are the scientists involved? What are they like? If the newspaper doesn't tell you, invent the characters yourself.

Copycat?

Rewriting a newspaper story does not make it your own. The writer or publisher has the **copyright** for the article. You don't have the right to copy what they have written, but you can take a real-life piece of news and draw information from it for a different story. You could turn the discovery of a dinosaur into a story about an archaeologist who digs up a dinosaur skeleton that comes to life after everyone at the museum has gone home. This turns **facts** into fiction.

Springboard

Take a few words from a newspaper article or headline and use them as a story title. You are only using the words for the title, so your story will be nothing like the one in the newspaper. Here are some made-up headlines to get you started:

- Prince pays the price
- Polly the parrot keeps quiet
- Cheesy does it!
- Smallest mammal discovered
- Rover to the rescue!

Tip

All stories involve a character, either human or animal, who has a problem that must be solved—a conflict. Before you start writing, ask yourself: Who is my story's main character and what is his or her conflict?

Tip

Change the characters' names from those in real life to something memorable. Professor Trudie Spligwort is quite a catchy name!

the daily news

NEW PLANET DISCOVERED

FROM FACT TO FICTION

It can be hard to get started with story writing. People often say, "Write about what you know." Writing from your own experience gives you confidence, but you can also describe what happens to others. Because your brain gathers knowledge from the world around you all the time, you don't need to have broken a bone yourself to have a character break a leg!

"I know..." plus "what if...?"

Here's a way to write a story that uses what you know to create what you can only imagine. Write an account of something that has happened in your life as if you were telling a friend or writing a diary. Read it through with a pen handy. Ask yourself "What if ...?" and then change some things slightly and others dramatically, turning facts into fiction. Maybe you could introduce a fantasy element. Here's an example:

Edit the text so that the narrative flows more smoothly.

This morning, when I opened the curtains the sky was green. My mouth fell open. ~~it was pouring with rain~~. ~~I was annoyed because~~ had planned a M my friend Danny and I ~~were planning a~~ picnic by the river. ~~Instead we decided to go to the movies.~~ but the voice that answered I called Danny, ~~and we arranged to meet at the~~ sounded nothing like him. ~~bus stop and get the twelve-thirty bus into town~~.

Check that your new words make sense alongside the original words that you're keeping.

Tip

In your writing, it is better to show than tell. For example, "I was annoyed" tells the reader how the author felt, but "My mouth fell open" is much more expressive. It shows that the author was astounded without actually saying it.

Copy the start of your new story onto a fresh sheet of paper, like this:

Springboard

In your story, try using the same words at the end of your story that you used at the beginning, such as:
- I never did like carrots.
- It was the first and last time I ever saw my cousin.
- Dogs understand more than we think.

This morning, when I opened the curtains, the sky was green. My mouth fell open. My friend Danny and I had planned a picnic by the river. I called Danny, but the voice that answered sounded nothing like him.

The story now has many possibilities. Danny sounds different.

- Will he look different, too?
- Has Danny turned into someone else?
- Is the sky really green and, if so, why? Or are the writer's senses confused?

Ask yourself "what," "where," "why," and "who" questions about your own story. Jot down ideas so that you know where the story is going and how it will end. Then write the rest of the story before your enthusiasm dwindles.

Springboard

- Imagine yourself shrinking or growing so that a familiar environment becomes threatening or dangerous.

- Have a fantasy character living your life. For example: What happens when a snowman eats oatmeal or sits next to the radiator at school?

9

BUILDING A STORY

Writing a story is a bit like building a house. You gather your materials—your words—but before you can begin building, you need a design. Here are the things you need for your story design:

Protagonist:
Drizzle the wizard
or Wikedelia
the witch?
Other characters:
Crumble the Cat
Freaky Frog
Elfrida
always mumbling under her breath; allergic to feathers?

Setting

The setting is the story's time and place. It could be another planet in the future, a school, or a pharaoh's palace. You may find it helps to imagine the setting as a theater. Picture a stage for your characters with several backdrops for different scenes.

TIME: 3,000 BCE
PLACE: Egypt
SCENES: The throne room of the Pharaoh's palace; a holy temple; the dark, winding halls of a pyramid; a barge on the Nile.

Characters

The main character is called the **protagonist**. Try to make your readers care about and identify with this person, which means being able to understand and share the character's thoughts and feelings. You can create characters that oppose the protagonist or influence events. Use **dialogue** to show characters' personalities. Picture them: How do they speak? What habits do they have?

Don't create too many characters for you or your readers to remember!

Theme

The theme is the story's message. It should be something that the reader thinks about after reading the story. For example, the theme may be "you can overcome fear" or "bad people don't win."

Plot

The events that take place, their order, their reason for occurring, and their outcome make up the **plot**. Making a time line helps you to work out the plot. Write the story's main events along the time line.

Kit goes on vacation

Feels bored and lonely

Meets magic horse

Kit and horse dive into ocean

They reach island

Kit meets pirates

Finds treasure

From start to finish

Once you have your story's setting, characters, and plot, it's time to start "building." Your story will have three parts: a beginning, a middle, and an end.

Beginning

Make the start of your story short. Involve the reader right away, but without too much description or detail. A good way to start is with **direct speech**.

"Hey–that's *my* bike you're riding," shouted Jack.
The girl wobbled for a second as she glanced over her shoulder.
"Well, it's *mine* now," she said.

We learn several things:
The main character is named Jack.
There's a confrontation and problem to overcome.
Jack may not know the girl. (The author hasn't used her name—yet!)

Middle

Next, the characters develop and things happen in a series of connected events. The characters' actions influence events, which may, in turn, change the characters' feelings, attitudes, or even their whole lives!

End

It is important to tie up "loose ends." Don't leave your reader thinking, "But what about such-and-such?" Provide a satisfying outcome. It must leave the protagonist (and readers who care about him or her) feeling better off than at the start and with most—if not all—problems solved. Readers should be able to close the book feeling content that they know what happened to all the characters.

Tip

A page of text could cover any amount of time, from a minute to half a lifetime, depending on the story length. Make the plot unfold fast enough to keep your readers' attention but slow enough for them to get to know the characters and share the action.

Springboard

Try building a story from these materials:

THEME: Lost SETTING: Fairground
PROTAGONIST: Young boy or girl
PLOT: Boy/girl has run away because he/she is unhappy. By the end of the story, the child is back home and the reader knows why the child was unhappy, how he or she was found, and why the child is happier than he or she was before.

CREATING CHARACTERS

Believable characters are vital to a good story. They should seem like real people, so remember that nobody is all good or all bad. Even the nastiest character might be kind to dogs or love their mother! Even the nicest has a weak spot—a streak of jealousy, maybe. You decide—but beware! As your characters become more real, it can be hard to make them stay in the plot.

> Creating a character is like making a new friend!

GRANDPA GREGOR'S CHARACTER FILE

Character file

Keep a fact-file about each key character. The more you include, the more you will get to know them. Include their coloring, age, height, build, hobbies, pets, favorite food, favorite sports team, or anything else of interest. You could also note their greatest disappointment or ambition. Once their personalities are established, the characters will seem real.

70 years old and frail; long, white hair; rimless glasses; usually bent over but straightens up when speaking. Listens to big band music on his MP3 player. Would like to have played the trombone.

Tip

Some friends may take offense to appearing in your stories, so if you base a character on someone you know, make sure to disguise them. If it's a boy, make him a girl, and so on. Change other details, such as their age, hair color, or height.

Showing emotion

People's facial expressions and body language reveal what they are feeling. Imagine your character. Then show, rather than tell (see page 8), your reader about the character's feelings through their actions, reactions, dialogue, and body language.

TELL: Raj was unhappy.
SHOW: Raj strolled slowly, his head down and shoulders hunched. He frowned hard and bit his lip.

Note: When showing, the adjective "unhappy" doesn't appear. Nor does the verb "cry," but we know Raj was close to tears!

Environment

Sometimes we learn about a character from their environment:

"The bedroom was messy but, nevertheless, had an orderliness about it. A pile of horse books on the floor beside the unmade bed were sorted by size. A caged hamster shared a bookshelf with a cuddly toy rabbit that had obviously been well squeezed for most of its owner's ten years. Shoved to the back of a small desk lay a half-written letter. The pile of dust it lay under suggested it was unlikely to see the inside of an envelope."

What's in a name?

Authors often pick names that reflect a character's looks or personality, such as Mr. Happy, Penny Sweet, or Old Mrs. Longtooth. Choose unusual names to make it easier for you—and your readers—to remember who's who. For example, Jeannie Blacklake is more memorable than Jane Black.

BRAINSTORMING

Everyone in the world has at least one story to tell. If you add up all of those imaginations, there are limitless ideas! Here are some ways of coming up with plots and planning how they will develop:

Brainstorming

Take a single word and write down absolutely anything relating to it. Give yourself just five minutes and *don't think too hard!*

Start with one of these words:
PAPER WALLS SPACE WATER

Choose one thought that you've come up with and do further **brainstorming** about it.

Now, think of an incident that involves one of your ideas. This incident can form part of a story, or you can develop the whole plot around it.

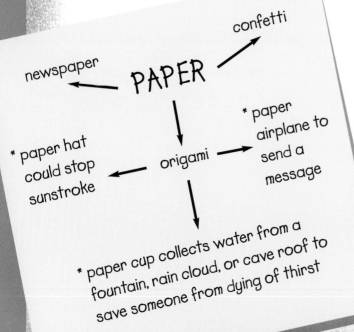

confetti

newspaper

PAPER

* paper hat could stop sunstroke

origami

* paper airplane to send a message

* paper cup collects water from a fountain, rain cloud, or cave roof to save someone from dying of thirst

Good planning

Creating problems and solving each one in turn makes for a good plot. As you plan your plot, you will see how, as in real life, there isn't always one "right" thing to do. Your characters will reach crossroads and have to choose a direction. Add a happy ending—even if there are tears along the way—or your readers will never forgive you!

What's the plot?

Plots usually involve one or both of the following:

- Thwarted ambition: Someone or something stops the hero from getting what they want. They want to get from A to B but there are obstacles in the way.
- An emotional issue: There is a problem that involves a person's feelings and affects their lives. The hero goes on a "personal journey" throughout the story. (This might also involve an actual journey to another place, such as a new home.)

Storyboarding

One helpful way to plan the plot is by **storyboarding**. Draw a series of boxes. Make one for each **paragraph**, if it's a short story; one for each **chapter** if it's a **novel**. In each box, sketch the main event, as if it was a scene in a movie. Use these pictures as a prompt for your writing. Or write notes to remind you what will happen at each stage of the story. For example, here is a storyboard for *Little Red Riding Hood*:

Springboard

Make a storyboard for your favorite story or fairy tale. You don't need to use full sentences, just briefly jot down—or sketch —the main events in order.

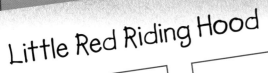

Little Red Riding Hood

Mother tells Little Red Riding Hood to put on cloak and take cake to Grandma who is sick in bed on other side of forest.	LRRH in wood, stops to picks flowers on way, not noticing a wolf spying on her.	Wolf asks where she is going. She tells him where and why, and he says good-bye and disappears.
LRRH arrives at G'ma's and finds her looking odd: eyes too big, ears too big; G'ma misleads her ("All the better to see / hear you with"). LRRH mentions G'ma's huge teeth.	G'ma says, "All the better to eat you with"–leaps from bed to attack LRRH who sees wolf is dressed up in G'ma's nightgown.	LRRH screams and her dad (who is a woodsman chopping down trees nearby) arrives with ax and kills wolf. They find G'ma shut in wardrobe.

DECISIONS, DECISIONS

Before you start writing, you must decide on a viewpoint (whether you are in the story—or not) and **tense** (whether you will be writing in the past or present tense).

Point of view

From whose viewpoint are you writing?

• You can be an observer, as if you were watching a film. If so, you will write in the "third person": *he, she, they, his, her,* and *their* are useful pronouns.

• You can write as one of the characters, as if you were inside the story. If so, you will be writing in the "first person": *I, me, my, we, us,* and *our* are useful pronouns.

Past or present?

Are you telling the story in the past or present tense?

• The past tense is the most common and perhaps the easiest way of storytelling: *He went… They chose… It was fun…*

• The present tense is less common but can be useful—especially as a contrast for a character relating an event or a dream: *I am… I choose… It is fun…*

TIP

Even if you are writing fantasy, it must be believable to your readers. Make up the "rules" for your fantasy world—and stick to them. If your character suddenly sprouts wings to escape from a lion, that's too easy a way out. On the other hand, the character could ride on the back of a winged creature to escape.

ACTIVITY

Read the opening lines of some stories you have enjoyed. What have the authors said, and how have they said it? Which viewpoint have they taken? Did they write in the past or present tense? Plan an opening sentence or paragraph that will grab your readers' attention. Rewrite it, changing the viewpoint and tense. How does it affect your writing's impact?

Symbols

Before you begin to write, you must also decide if you will use **symbols** in your story. Symbols are things that stand for something. Colors are often used as symbols. For example, the color red may symbolize danger. In *Little Red Riding Hood,* her red cloak warns the reader of trouble ahead. Symbols are not always colors. For example, a dove is a symbol of peace and love, like the dove in *Noah's Ark.*

Animal symbols

Animals often symbolize human character types—a lion is usually bold, a peacock, proud, and so on. You can use them in stories to reinforce the type of character they are. Or you can make them behave the opposite of their stereotype, like the nervous lion in *The Wizard of Oz* or Kenneth Grahame's gentle, friendly *Reluctant Dragon.*

Weather symbols

Weather that echoes a character's feelings can be used to create atmosphere. If your hero is unhappy, rain might reflect that sadness, just as sunshine could reflect a character's happiness and joy. Fog could reinforce a character's feelings of being lost or confused.

Select one of the titles below or make up your own. Then choose some symbols around which to plan the story.

- Red Snow
- The Lion Who Was Afraid
- Bottled Sunshine

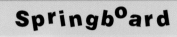
Springboard

The Cat and the Broomstick

Black Hat Stories

Rainy Day Spells

ACTIVITY

Use weather or animal symbols in a fantasy story, such as one about a talking animal, a superhero, or an underground world that nobody's discovered before. Try writing *The Country Where the Sun Never Shone.* Why doesn't it shine? Who arrives to change all that?

PACE AND TIMING

Stories are often about journeys, either from place to place or through time. There are also emotional and personal journeys taken as characters deal with events. **Pace** and timing are useful tools for inviting the reader to join the journey.

The journey starts

It's a good idea to estimate how many words your story will be before you start. Then you can decide how many words to use to set the scene and introduce the characters. If your story will be 1,000 words long in total, the beginning will probably be no more than 200 words.

Setting the pace

Deciding how to divide up the text across a whole piece of writing is called pacing. It is not good to write a lot of detail for the first three-quarters of your story and then have to hurry the story along at the end.

Speed up and slow down

Pace also refers to how you tell the story. Vary the pace of your storytelling to avoid sounding boring.

ACTIVITY

Write two different openings to a story with a maximum of 200 words each.

1. Introduce the main character, starting with his or her birth. Include something remarkable, such as being born in a strange place. By the end, the character is 12 years old and in the here and now.

2. The character is 12 years old already. It could be an ordinary day that becomes extraordinary or a special day from the start. Help the reader find out as much as possible about the character.

How do the things we learn about the character differ between the first and second version? Which is more detailed? Are there more of the character's thoughts and feelings in the second?

- Long sentences with **subclauses** and commas slow down the story.
- Words with long vowel sounds—such as *oa*, *ee*, and *ai*—also relax the pace.
- Short sentences or phrases speed up the pace and add excitement.

The long and short of it

Read these two paragraphs. Each contains just 42 words, but the first covers more than 60 years while the other covers fewer than 60 seconds.

In sixty years, I had crossed every continent. I allowed my gaze to wander the length and depth of the wide, blue sky. Every vapor trail seemed to lead away from me, far away to the distant horizon, inviting me to follow.

Suddenly there was a bang on the roof. There was a crash right above my head. I yelped. A flash of orange outside the window made me recoil. My throat tightened. I struggled to swallow. "It can't be!" I croaked. But it was.

Tip
When you describe things, try to involve all five senses: touch, sight, sound, taste, and smell.

Time phrases

A way of showing the passage of time is to use a time **phrase**. "Shortly" and "soon" mean almost the same thing, but varying the phrases you use will spice up your writing. Here are some useful time phrases:

- soon
- shortly
- it was some time before
- before long
- meanwhile
- within the hour
- two weeks later
- after a while
- the following afternoon
- the next day
- until then
- in the next few days

- at first
- at last
- suddenly
- all at once
- just at that moment
- long ago
- as fast as
- for a second
- while
- during
- no sooner had... than...

Springboard

Write a story based on one of these journeys:

- Through the tunnel
- Over the rainbow
- Below the surface

Include at least one unusual form of transportation—anything from a camel train to a parachute.

BREAKING WRITER'S BLOCK

Have you ever sat down to write and found that your brain wouldn't join in? You had no idea what to write, and your mind was a blank. All writers get this from time to time. It's called writer's block. Here are some ideas to help you get going if you feel blocked:

Better late than never

A fool and his/her money are soon parted

Absence makes the heart grow fonder

Choose a **proverb** or saying and plan a story that proves its truth. Here are some to start you off...

Where there's a will, there's a way

Never, never, never

Parents and teachers tell us things that we MUST NOT do! Brainstorm a "never" list, for example:

NEVER TELL ANYONE ABOUT THE TIGER

NEVER TOUCH THE RED BUTTON

NEVER GO THROUGH THE GREEN GATE

NEVER PICK UP A SPOTTED SNAIL

Choose one of these warnings and decide what happens when your main character ignores it!

Disaster!

In real life, stories often revolve around an accident or a mistake. Describe an accident that happened to you or one you caused. It can be as small as tripping over a shoelace or dropping a take-out meal, or as big as a car crash or falling off a swing. Add a little imagination and poetic license (the author's "right" to change things slightly). Can you develop it into a story?

Or try one of these titles*:

- A Broken Ankle
- Cat Catastrophe
- Mistaken Identity
- The Forgotten Letter
- Wrong Time; Wrong Place

* These are working titles—a title you give your story while you are writing it. It's often best to choose the final title when your story is complete. It should be one that intrigues people, making them want to read your story, but without giving too much away.

Tip

When developing an idea, try to think as widely as possible of ways of interpreting your seed of an idea so that it will grow beautifully. Use an idea web to brainstorm.

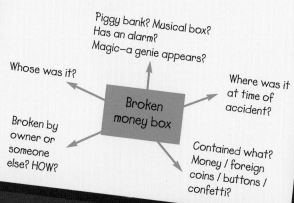

Piggy bank? Musical box? Has an alarm? Magic—a genie appears?

Whose was it?

Where was it at time of accident?

Broken money box

Broken by owner or someone else? HOW?

Contained what? Money / foreign coins / buttons / confetti?

Springboard

Try automatic writing. It's writing in which you pick up your pen and write whatever comes into your head. You might even start by writing the same word over and over until another pops into your head. The point is you ARE writing and—like an artist sketching before painting—a part of your automatic writing may grow into a story.

STORIES WITH CHAPTERS

Short stories are fun to write—but how about a novel or **novella**? Here are some of the good things about writing a longer story.

You can...

- develop characters in greater depth, until they seem as real as your friends.
- take your characters through more experiences and to more locations.
- further describe the setting and create different moods to complement the action.

One way to start...

If the idea of writing a novel seems scary, try writing a series of short stories about one character with a plot thread that links the stories. Join them as chapters in one book to create an **episodic** novel. Make sure that the plot is resolved in the final chapter.

For example, you might have a character who plays pranks on people. Each chapter—a story in its own right—talks about a trick he's played. At the same time, all those who were tricked prepare to get him back. They build up their friendship and plan revenge. The story reaches a climax as the joker is tricked in return.

ACTIVITY

Create a character with a problem— such as a girl who is struggling with homework. In trying to solve her problem, she creates a second one and so on. For example, her friend spills orange juice on both their books. In the next chapter, they wipe their books with a bleach-soaked cloth. So they accidentally bleach the sofa. This type of thing continues until the final chapter, in which all of the problems are solved.

Tip

If you use a computer word-processing program to write, it makes it easy to cut and paste text. This means you can add a chapter in the middle of the book, if you want, without having to rewrite anything.

Chapter know-how

As you add more detail to any story, it will get longer, so you can divide it into chapters. Make sure each chapter ends with a cliff-hanger—a situation that makes the reader want to turn the page and read more. The start of each chapter must grab the reader's attention, too, just as the very first line of the story did.

Springboard

Plan and write a story in five chapters using the titles below. Don't forget the cliff-hangers!

Chapter 1   A Step Too Far
Chapter 2   Waiting
Chapter 3   What a Find!
Chapter 4   Many Hands Make Light Work
Chapter 5   Just Rewards

ACTIVITY

Can you write a chapter that ends with one of these cliff-hangers?

- When at last he woke, all he saw were stars in the purple sky above.
- There was only one thing to do: She would have to jump.
- Four more days of this!
- It was now or never. I took a deep breath and knocked on the door.

When you have finished, try to write the next chapter. Make sure the ending is a cliff-hanger.

PINK PIANO FOR SALE

Made especially for the Intergalactic Musical Instrument Exhibition, this UNIQUE PINK PIANO is like no piano on Earth.

All offers considered—BUY IT NOW and discover its amazing musical effects on your next trip to the Red Planet!

Purple Sky Seen By All

Springboard

Now try a six-chapter book linking these chapter titles:

Chapter 1   The Pink Piano
Chapter 2   A Strange Teacher
Chapter 3   Making Excuses
Chapter 4   Music on Mars
Chapter 5   A Missing Note
Chapter 6   Home Again

CONNECT THE DOTS

See how good you are at plotting a story that has to include certain, unconnected words at least once each.

These two story plans include each word from the list on the right. Both plans link the words into a story line, but in a different order.

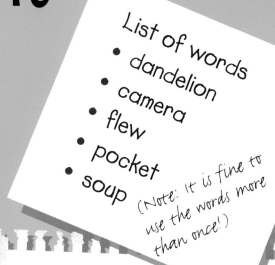

List of words
- dandelion
- camera
- flew
- pocket
- soup

(Note: It is fine to use the words more than once!)

Plan 1

Mom asks you to pick dandelion leaves for salad. Pick a few—gets boring. Start blowing dandelion heads. Seeds fly over next-door neighbor's fence. Old lady next door angry—doesn't want weeds in her veg patch—marches over to your mom. Mom invites old lady to stay for lunch. Old lady (Maud) delighted—says looks too good to eat: pulls camera out of pocket & photographs it before enjoying eating. Next day Maud comes over with homegrown leeks & potatoes. Digs recipe for leek & potato soup out of her pocket. You decide to cook it for dinner. You take photograph of finished soup. Ending: You, Mom & Maud share more recipes & create Community Cook Book—raises money for senior citizen's center (Maud said she is lonely.)

Plan 2

Outdoor picnic. Something looking like dandelion seed flies into cup of soup. Starts to grow. Shock! Amazement! Grab camera to photograph it as it quickly grows. See woman walking by—struggling with her coat as seed begins growing in her pocket. Same everywhere. Seeds growing in unlikely places. Young plants sprout legs & jump out, running in one direction. Everyone follows, huge spaceship descends, green creatures enter it. Disappears in space. People left dumbfounded—except central character. He/she has one last seedling: a miniature alien to keep as a pet/secret friend named…Dandelion!

(Note: This one is briefer; details need to be added.)

Note that one story is realistic, the other fantasy; but both started with the same list of words.

ACTIVITY

Choose a set of words from below. Write each word on a piece of paper and shuffle them.

- Let one or two words suggest the beginning of a story—a setting, character, or event.
- Make brief notes as ideas come to you, perhaps using an idea web.
- Develop your notes into a simple story plan. These are the "dots" that you will connect as you write your story.

Now "connect the dots" by thinking up an attention-grabbing start to your story and then continue writing to the end.

Tip

There's no need to use full sentences in your story plan!

Set 1. bone sneezed window suitcase onions

Set 2. drum valuable spoon swam magnet

Set 3. helicopter address butterfly sunset danced giraffe

Set 4. box bald mountain enormous circle purple

Set 5. arrow rainbow owl middle castle hungry safe

Set 6. trip lake dragon peaceful party tore twenty abandoned

Set 7. Saturday damaged lonely ice guitar growl danced chicken

Tip

If there is a word that seems tricky to fit in, use an idea web to help you.

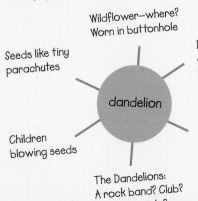

Wildflower—where?
Worn in buttonhole

Seeds like tiny parachutes

Dandelion: name of...pet? place? boat?

dandelion

Children blowing seeds

Edible leaves— eaten in salads; also loved by rabbits and guinea pigs

The Dandelions: A rock band? Club? Secret society?

Springboard

- Think up more word lists to inspire "connect-the-dots" stories and trade them with your friends.
- Ask your family members to give you one word each. Combine the words into a list.
- Play a word-building game (such as Scrabble®) or do a crossword puzzle. Then choose six of the words for your word list.

STORY MAPPING

Remember to decide early on from whose viewpoint you will tell the story.

Sometimes a writer's head can be buzzing with ideas. How do you decide which idea to develop from a number of different ones that all seem good? There's a way to sort out all your ideas and choose which ones to include and which to throw out. It's called a story map.

A story map makes it much easier to make sense of your ideas. Every time you make a decision, your story changes direction. You end up writing a different story from what it would have been if you had made a different choice. Look at the story map on the next page. A boy is going on vacation with his family. Where are they going and how are they getting there? Something unexpected is going to happen.

ACTIVITY

Follow the arrows from the top of the story map on the next page to choose a story route. Write each choice on a sheet of paper. When you reach a question mark, use your imagination to make up the end of the story. When you have finished, you can draw a storyboard (see page 15) to decide the order of events.

At this point, you can alter the order in which you describe events to the reader.

For example, you might begin your story with the boy knocking on a small cottage door. The cottage belongs to somebody whose phone number he called earlier, when he found it in the glove compartment of the taxi. (You can explain why the family called a taxi later in the story.) This allows you to grab the reader's attention with an exciting part of the plot, drawing them into the story right from page one.

Springboard

Try finishing this story map and see where it leads.

IN THE JUNGLE
Two friends carrying backpacks are heading down a jungle path.

One begins to climb up a vine, like climbing a rope.

One sits down on a log for a drink.

The person looks down to see a snake is climbing up, too.

?

?

His or her backpack starts to shake violently.

THE VACATION

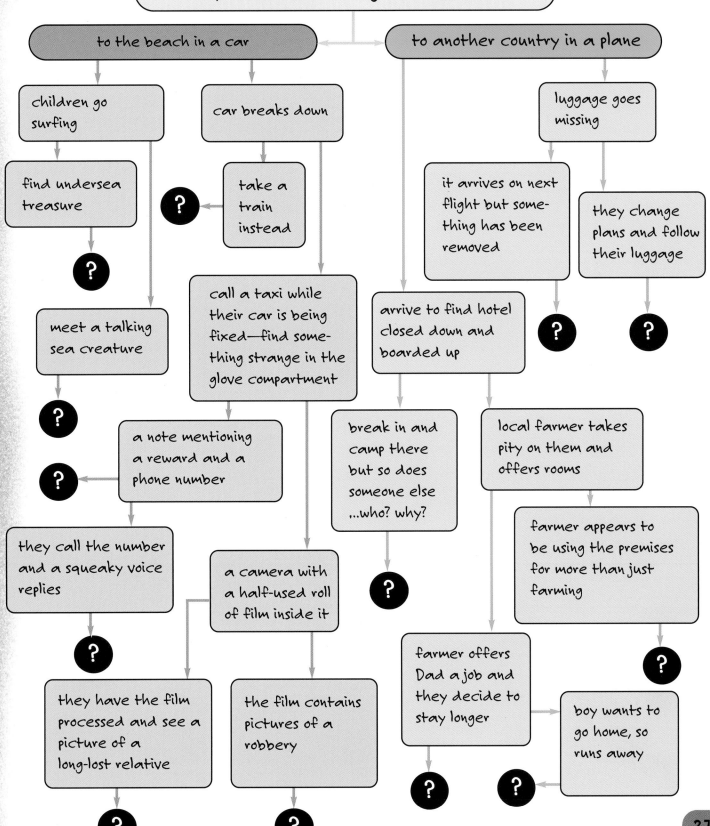

Boy, sister, parents go on vacation

to the beach in a car

to another country in a plane

children go surfing

car breaks down

luggage goes missing

find undersea treasure

take a train instead

?

it arrives on next flight but something has been removed

they change plans and follow their luggage

?

meet a talking sea creature

call a taxi while their car is being fixed—find something strange in the glove compartment

arrive to find hotel closed down and boarded up

?

?

?

a note mentioning a reward and a phone number

break in and camp there but so does someone else ...who? why?

local farmer takes pity on them and offers rooms

?

they call the number and a squeaky voice replies

a camera with a half-used roll of film inside it

farmer appears to be using the premises for more than just farming

?

?

they have the film processed and see a picture of a long-lost relative

the film contains pictures of a robbery

farmer offers Dad a job and they decide to stay longer

?

boy wants to go home, so runs away

?

?

?

?

SUMMING UP

Planning characters, setting, plot, opening lines, viewpoint—what a lot of things an author has to weave together to create a story! The main thing is to stick with it. Keep practicing!

Writing reminders

Here are some things to remember when writing stories.

• Make sure first lines grab attention.

• Show rather than tell.

• Experiment with different voices—write as different characters.

• Use dialogue to break up narrative.

• Read aloud and rewrite to improve the flow.

• Use the five senses in descriptions.

• Vary your sentence length to change pace.

• Tie up loose ends before the close of your story.

• Create a happy ending—satisfying for the reader.

• End chapters with a page-turning cliff-hanger.

• "Proofread" your story:
  • Do all pronouns agree with their subjects?
  • Is your continuity of action accurate?
  • Have you overused certain words?
  • Have you checked the spelling?
  • Is your use of tense consistent?

What next?

Now that your writing is finished, here are some things to do with it:

• Start a writers' club with like-minded friends. Read your stories to each other. Give and take helpful critiques (constructive, critical comments on your writing). No author ever stops learning how to improve!

• Produce a short story **anthology** with your friends, containing a story by each of you.

• Desktop publish your stories—adding illustrations—on your computer. You could staple them together to create a whole library of your own books!

- Get together with friends to publish a magazine for other friends and family to enjoy.

- Find writing competitions to enter. These are often advertised in libraries and bookstores. Some appear on Web sites—but check who is running them first. Are they a well-established publisher or arts group? Do they have a children's section? Do they have young people free to enter? Ask an adult for help.

Springboard 1

Try developing any of these ideas as stories:

Something appears... in the steam of the kettle... through the window... in the mirror... on the computer... or a presenter speaks to you from the TV screen... WHAT HAPPENS NEXT?

Springboard 2

A child helps an elderly person who has fallen down. What happens next? Maybe the two find that they have something unlikely in common, such as odd socks or a pet goldfish. Perhaps the elderly person gives the child a reward—where does that lead them next?

Springboard 3

You find a ball. When it bounces it does something magical—it always goes where you kick or throw it; it glows and hums and an alien emerges; or it bursts like a balloon and suddenly snow falls in summer? Think of a reason to explain the magical event. For example, snow might help penguins that are overheating in the local zoo.

GLOSSARY

Anthology   collection of stories by different authors

Author   person who writes a book

Brainstorm   to think of anything and everything related to one subject

Chapter   a division of text within a longer narrative; one section of a book

Character   a fictional person in a book

Copyright   the author's or publisher's right of ownership to original text

Dialogue   direct speech between characters

Direct speech   writing words as spoken ("I love you," he said.)

Edit   to alter or rewrite, often removing or replacing words

Episodic   written in episodes (parts) which describe a series of events

Fable   a legendary story not based on fact, often with a moral or a message

Facts   things that are true rather than imaginary or made-up

Fantasy   imaginary creation that could never be real

Fiction   created from the imagination; not true or factual

Genre   type of writing with a specific style and purpose

Legend   a traditional historical story sometimes believed to be fact but without factual evidence

Narrative   another word for story

Novel   an extended story, usually divided into chapters

Novella   a short novel

Pace   the speed at which the action happens

Paragraph   a division within a piece of writing that contains several sentences on a similar theme or subject matter

Phrase   a group of words

Plot   plan of a sequence of connected events with an outcome developed from the start

Protagonist   central character or hero to whom the reader can relate

Proverb   a saying with a moral to it that offers advice by sharing a human experience

Sentence   a series of words that make sense and include a verb (an action word)

Storyboard   to plan a story using a picture sequence of the main scenes

Subclause   a phrase within a sentence, separated by commas on each side

Symbol   something that represents an idea or meaning beyond itself

Tense   the form a verb takes to indicate past, present, or future (such as was, is, will be)

Text   the words on the page

INDEX

NOTES FOR PARENTS AND TEACHERS

- Children are natural storytellers. Watch them at the playground planning the characters, scenario, and events of an imaginary world—they are never short of ideas. As they get older, many children will happily develop from storytellers to writers. Others may need encouragement. This book aims to help children start writing and stick with it. They will see their story ideas grow from seeds into plants. Nothing succeeds like success.

- This book aims to encourage and improve the art of storytelling. It gives ideas and advice. Its main purpose is to persuade children to "let go" and really develop their art. At first, this may be at the expense of things such as spelling. Do not worry too much about this. The main thing is that the child is getting his or her ideas down on paper. There is plenty of time later to correct spelling, punctuation, and so forth. In fact, proofreading and rewriting are discussed in this book.

- You can help your children in many ways. Always be willing to read their stories—but only when they ask you to do so. Never pressure them to tell you what they are writing about or how it will end. They may not know until after they've written it!

- When you do read their story, they will be dying to know what you think of it. Mainly—did you enjoy it? Always find something positive to say that will encourage your child to continue writing. Anyone, young or old, will improve at an art the more they practice it. They can discover for themselves how much progress they've made as time goes by. Encourage them to keep examples of their early efforts so that they will be able to see their improvement.

- Be prepared to offer children help if they ask for it. They may come up against frustrating plot issues that hadn't occurred to them and are spoiling the rest of their story. (A penguin is crucial to the plot and the setting is a desert!) It may be that, through discussion, they can find a way around their problem. (Make it a vulture instead of a penguin or move the setting to the Antarctic!)

- Do not mock your child's efforts—even if they are humorous when they're not meant to be. Feelings are easily hurt.

- Even struggling readers and children with literacy difficulties have creative minds. If your child is bursting with ideas, but struggles to get them down on paper, offer to act as a secretary—write the words he or she dictates. Alternatively, encourage him or her to use a voice recorder and help transcribe the story.